PRINCEWILL LAGANG

The Musk Effect: Unravelling the Dogecoin Phenomenon and Its Impact on Digital Finance in 2025

First published by Lagang Princewill 2025

Copyright © 2025 by Princewill Lagang

All rights reserved. No part of this publication may be reproduced, stored or transmitted in any form or by any means, electronic, mechanical, photocopying, recording, scanning, or otherwise without written permission from the publisher. It is illegal to copy this book, post it to a website, or distribute it by any other means without permission.

Princewill Lagang asserts the moral right to be identified as the author of this work.

First edition

This book was professionally typeset on Reedsy.
Find out more at reedsy.com

Contents

1	Introduction	1
2	The Birth of Dogecoin	3
3	Elon Musk Enters the Scene	5
4	The Power of Social Media and Musk Influence	7
5	Dogecoin as a Meme Coin	9
6	The Dogecoin Community	11
7	From Joke to Investment Opportunity	13
8	The Technology Behind Dogecoin	15
9	Musk, Dogecoin and the Rise of DeFi	17
10	The Volatility of Dogecoin	19
11	Dogecoin in 2025: Where are we now?	21
12	The Future of Digital Finance	23
13	The Musk Effect: What We've Learned	25
14	Conclusion	27

1

Introduction

Over the past decade, the world of cryptocurrencies has emerged as a groundbreaking force in finance, and at the forefront of this shift stands Elon Musk. As the CEO of Tesla and SpaceX, Musk has always been known for pushing the boundaries of technology and innovation. However, his influence extends far beyond electric cars and space exploration, reaching into the world of digital currencies. His often-controversial statements and actions regarding cryptocurrencies, particularly Dogecoin, have made him a central figure in this new economic era. Musk's involvement has not only shaped the trajectory of Dogecoin but has also played a significant role in defining the cryptocurrency landscape itself.

Dogecoin's journey is unique within the cryptocurrency market. What initially began as a lighthearted joke, inspired by an internet meme featuring a Shiba Inu dog, has evolved into one of the most recognizable and widely traded cryptocurrencies in the world. While Bitcoin and Ethereum have long dominated the space, Dogecoin's meteoric rise can largely be attributed to Musk's support and the viral nature of his endorsements. From tweets to public endorsements, Musk has demonstrated the power of social media and celebrity influence in driving market trends. This book will delve into how Dogecoin, with its meme origins, captured the attention of millions, evolving from a niche digital currency into a global phenomenon with real-world impact.

As we approach 2025, the cryptocurrency market continues to grow and change at an exponential rate. Dogecoin's rise, fueled by Musk's engagement, highlights not only the potential of digital currencies but also the inherent volatility that accompanies them. In this book, we will examine the broader implications of cryptocurrencies on the global financial system, the role of influencers like Musk in shaping market behavior, and the future of digital currencies in a world where innovation and speculation collide. By exploring Dogecoin's unlikely path to prominence, we can gain valuable insights into the dynamic relationship between technology, finance, and culture in the age of cryptocurrencies.

2

The Birth of Dogecoin

Chapter 1:

Dogecoin's story began in 2013 when two software engineers, Billy Markus and Jackson Palmer, sought to create a cryptocurrency that stood out from the burgeoning digital finance landscape. Unlike Bitcoin, which was often portrayed as serious and revolutionary, Markus and Palmer envisioned a coin that embraced humor and community. Their inspiration came from a viral meme featuring a Shiba Inu dog with amusing captions written in broken English. The meme's quirky charm embodied the lightheartedness they wanted their project to represent. With this mascot as its emblem, Dogecoin was born—a playful counterpoint to the sometimes intimidating and technical world of cryptocurrency.

What started as a tongue-in-cheek experiment quickly gained traction within the online community. Dogecoin's approachable and inclusive nature attracted enthusiasts who valued its simplicity and fun-loving ethos. The coin's launch coincided with a growing interest in blockchain technology and an explosion of internet culture, which provided fertile ground for its popularity. Dogecoin's users embraced its humorous origins, creating memes, sponsoring charitable campaigns, and even funding sports teams. This unique blend of financial technology and internet culture set Dogecoin apart, transforming it into a cultural phenomenon.

The rise of Dogecoin took an even more dramatic turn with the attention of high-profile figures, most notably Elon Musk. Musk's tongue-in-cheek tweets and public endorsements elevated the coin's visibility, drawing in a wave of new investors and further cementing its place in popular culture. What began as a joke had evolved into a legitimate digital asset, with a passionate community and a growing influence in the broader cryptocurrency market. Dogecoin's journey from meme to mainstream illustrates the unpredictable nature of innovation and the power of community in shaping modern finance.

3

Elon Musk Enters the Scene

Chapter 2:

Elon Musk's initial interaction with Dogecoin dates back to 2018, when he first mentioned the cryptocurrency on Twitter. While his early tweet—a simple nod to Dogecoin's existence—generated some buzz, it was relatively low-key compared to the phenomenon that would follow. At that time, Dogecoin was largely viewed as a niche project, a playful experiment within the cryptocurrency world. Musk's casual acknowledgment, however, planted a seed. For a man known for disrupting industries and engaging with his audience in unorthodox ways, this tweet marked the beginning of a relationship that would later transform Dogecoin from an internet curiosity into a mainstream topic.

Fast forward to 2021, and Musk's influence on Dogecoin took a dramatic turn.

Through a series of strategic and often humorous tweets, he propelled the cryptocurrency into the spotlight. Memes became his tool of choice, blending entertainment with subtle promotion. Posts like "Dogecoin is the people's crypto" resonated widely, sparking interest from seasoned investors and newcomers alike. His playful yet persuasive approach demystified the world of cryptocurrency, making it accessible and appealing to a broader audience. Each tweet or meme from Musk sent Dogecoin's value soaring, often leading to unprecedented market volatility. His tweets turned into events, eagerly anticipated by millions who saw him not just as a tech billionaire but as an unexpected champion of a decentralized, community-driven currency.

Musk's endorsement of Dogecoin also redefined its purpose. What began as a joke cryptocurrency evolved into a symbol of financial inclusivity and grassroots empowerment. By engaging with Dogecoin in a lighthearted manner, Musk made investing feel less intimidating, encouraging everyday people to participate. Beyond the memes and price surges, his influence fostered a sense of camaraderie among Dogecoin enthusiasts, uniting them under a shared vision of fun and possibility. While critics questioned the sustainability of this approach, there was no denying Musk's role in elevating Dogecoin from obscurity to cultural prominence, creating a lasting impact on the cryptocurrency landscape.

4

The Power of Social Media and Musk Influence

Chapter 3: Elon Musk's impact on Dogecoin exemplifies the extraordinary power social media wields in shaping public perception and market behavior. Through a series of tweets, Musk turned a relatively obscure cryptocurrency into a global sensation. His online presence and ability to connect with millions of followers made Dogecoin more than just a digital asset; it became a cultural phenomenon. Musk's playful engagement—from sharing memes to declaring Dogecoin as "the people's crypto"—ignited a surge of interest among investors and enthusiasts. This chapter examines the mechanisms behind Musk's influence, showing how his online persona and strategic communication amplified Dogecoin's reach and value.

The dynamics of Musk's influence are deeply rooted in his reputation as an innovative and visionary leader. As the CEO of companies like Tesla and SpaceX, Musk has cultivated an image of boldness and irreverence, which resonates with his followers. When Musk tweets about a topic, it creates a ripple effect: his statements are widely shared, dissected, and acted upon. In Dogecoin's case, Musk's tweets often led to immediate spikes in its market value, underscoring how celebrity endorsements can transcend traditional marketing. Social media platforms, particularly Twitter, acted as amplifiers, enabling Musk's messages to reach diverse audiences—from casual users to institutional investors—instantly and globally.

Dogecoin's rise, fueled by Musk's influence, highlights the intersection of social media, celebrity culture, and cryptocurrency. The meme-inspired token became a symbol of internet culture's power to disrupt traditional financial systems. Musk's playful engagement blurred the lines between entertainment and investment, making Dogecoin accessible to younger, tech-savvy demographics. However, this phenomenon also raises questions about market volatility and the ethical implications of such influence. As we explore the Dogecoin case, it becomes evident that Musk's role reflects a broader trend: social media's ability to democratize financial conversations while simultaneously magnifying risks in an increasingly interconnected digital world.

5

Dogecoin as a Meme Coin

Chapter 4:

Dogecoin, often labeled a "meme coin," represents a unique cultural and financial phenomenon within the cryptocurrency landscape. The term "meme coin" describes cryptocurrencies that originate primarily from internet culture, often as jokes or parodies, and derive their value largely from community enthusiasm rather than traditional financial metrics or utility. Dogecoin's journey began in 2013 as a lighthearted spoof of Bitcoin, combining the burgeoning interest in blockchain technology with the viral appeal of the Shiba Inu "Doge" meme. Despite its humorous beginnings, Dogecoin resonated with users who appreciated its playful nature and accessibility, ultimately leading to its rise as the archetypal meme coin.

Dogecoin's success can be attributed to several key factors, including its strong online community, low transaction fees, and widespread recognition as a "coin for the people." Unlike other cryptocurrencies that emphasize complex use cases or exclusivity, Dogecoin's simplicity and humor helped it capture the imagination of casual users and investors. Its community embraced the coin as a symbol of internet creativity, using it for small-scale tipping on social platforms and charitable endeavors. Over time, Dogecoin's unpretentious appeal created a loyal following that propelled its market presence far beyond its creators' initial expectations.

A major turning point for Dogecoin came with the public endorsement of influential figures, most notably Elon Musk. Musk's tweets and statements about Dogecoin elevated its visibility, injecting it with newfound legitimacy and sparking significant market activity. While critics argued that the coin's meteoric rise was unsustainable, Musk's influence demonstrated how cultural relevance and celebrity backing could reshape perceptions of value within the cryptocurrency market. As a result, Dogecoin transitioned from a niche internet joke to a digital asset with tangible economic impact, embodying both the power and unpredictability of meme culture in modern finance.

6

The Dogecoin Community

Chapter 5:

Behind every successful cryptocurrency lies a dedicated community of believers, and Dogecoin's journey is a testament to the power of collective enthusiasm. From its inception as a parody of the burgeoning crypto world, Dogecoin quickly attracted a unique following. Unlike other cryptocurrency communities that often focus on technological advancements or financial gain, the Dogecoin community stands out for its humor, generosity, and inclusivity. This group, bound by a shared appreciation for the coin's lighthearted origins, has cultivated an environment that welcomes both newcomers and seasoned investors alike. Their commitment has transcended financial transactions, creating a culture of camaraderie and mutual support.

The community's impact goes beyond fostering a sense of belonging; it has played a pivotal role in Dogecoin's growth and relevance. Social media platforms such as Reddit and Twitter serve as hubs where enthusiasts share memes, technical advice, and philanthropic initiatives. Notably, the community has organized numerous charitable efforts, including raising funds for clean water projects and sponsoring underdog athletes. These acts of goodwill have amplified Dogecoin's visibility, reinforcing its reputation as the "people's cryptocurrency." Such efforts demonstrate how a decentralized currency can inspire collective action, making Dogecoin not just an investment, but a movement.

One of the most influential figures within the Dogecoin community is Elon Musk, whose tweets and public endorsements have significantly bolstered the coin's popularity. Musk's quirky persona and fondness for memes resonate deeply with the Dogecoin ethos, cementing his status as a beloved figure. His involvement has attracted mainstream attention, drawing in both casual observers and serious investors. While his influence has sparked debates about market manipulation, there's no denying that Musk's association with Dogecoin has propelled it into the global spotlight. The synergy between Musk's playful engagement and the community's spirited dedication illustrates the unique dynamics that have made Dogecoin more than just a cryptocurrency; it's a cultural phenomenon.

7

From Joke to Investment Opportunity

C hapter 6:

In the dynamic world of cryptocurrency, Dogecoin stands out as a story of unexpected transformation. Originally created in 2013 as a lighthearted response to the burgeoning world of digital currencies, Dogecoin was inspired by the popular "Doge" meme, featuring a Shiba Inu dog with humorous captions in Comic Sans font. Its founders, Billy Markus and Jackson Palmer, intended it to be a playful alternative to the more serious and complex Bitcoin. With its comical origins and an enthusiastic online community, Dogecoin became a cultural phenomenon rather than a financial asset, thriving on the shared humor and camaraderie of its supporters.

However, Dogecoin's journey from joke to investment opportunity was set in motion by a combination of grassroots enthusiasm and market forces. Over time, its growing community began to use Dogecoin for charitable causes and tipping content creators online, showcasing its potential as a medium of exchange. The cryptocurrency's accessibility, low transaction fees, and active online following turned it into a symbol of digital inclusivity. This grassroots momentum caught the attention of high-profile figures, including tech billionaire Elon Musk, whose tweets about Dogecoin significantly boosted its visibility and market value. Suddenly, what began as a playful project was drawing the interest of mainstream investors and financial analysts.

The meteoric rise of Dogecoin's market value solidified its status as a legitimate digital asset. By early 2021, its price surged by thousands of percentage points, driven by a mix of social media hype, celebrity endorsements, and speculative trading. Investors who once dismissed it as a novelty began reconsidering its potential as a store of value or speculative investment. This shift underscores a broader trend in the cryptocurrency market, where even unconventional assets can gain serious traction. Dogecoin's ascent demonstrates the unpredictable nature of financial innovation, highlighting how humor, community, and technology can converge to create a powerful investment narrative.

8

The Technology Behind Dogecoin

Chapter 7:

Dogecoin, despite its playful origins as a meme-inspired cryptocurrency, operates on robust blockchain technology similar to Bitcoin. At its core, Dogecoin relies on a decentralized ledger, where every transaction is recorded transparently and securely. This ledger is maintained by a network of computers, or nodes, spread across the globe. The blockchain ensures that no single entity controls the network, which enhances its security and resilience. Dogecoin's structure is based on the Scrypt algorithm, an alternative to Bitcoin's SHA-256, which allows for faster transaction processing and lower energy consumption.

Transactions on the Dogecoin network are validated through a process known as mining. Miners use computational power to solve complex mathematical problems, which confirm the legitimacy of transactions and add them to the blockchain. This process also generates new Dogecoins as rewards for miners, ensuring the continuous supply of the cryptocurrency. Dogecoin's block time is significantly faster than Bitcoin's, taking approximately one minute to process a block compared to Bitcoin's ten minutes. This speed makes Dogecoin an attractive option for small, everyday transactions and contributes to its popularity for tipping and charitable donations within online communities.

One of the key distinctions between Dogecoin and other cryptocurrencies like Bitcoin and Ethereum lies in its approach to supply and utility. Unlike Bitcoin, which has a capped supply of 21 million coins, Dogecoin has an uncapped supply, allowing for infinite production. This design keeps transaction fees low and discourages hoarding. Compared to Ethereum, Dogecoin lacks the advanced functionalities of smart contracts and decentralized applications, focusing instead on simplicity and accessibility. While Bitcoin is often viewed as digital gold and Ethereum as a platform for decentralized innovation, Dogecoin has carved its niche as a user-friendly, community-driven cryptocurrency.

9

Musk, Dogecoin and the Rise of DeFi

Chapter 8:

The evolution of decentralized finance (DeFi) has reshaped the global financial landscape, presenting opportunities for financial autonomy and innovation beyond the confines of traditional banking systems. Within this dynamic space, Dogecoin, initially conceived as a parody of cryptocurrencies, has emerged as an unexpected player, partly due to Elon Musk's vocal support. Musk's influence, often amplified through social media, has propelled Dogecoin from a niche community to mainstream attention, showcasing the role of individual advocacy in the DeFi revolution. This chapter delves into the synergy between Musk's endorsement of Dogecoin and the broader goals of DeFi, illuminating how a meme-inspired cryptocurrency has sparked significant discourse about decentralization and accessibility in finance.

Dogecoin's unique position in the DeFi ecosystem lies in its ability to simplify complex financial concepts for a broad audience. Unlike other cryptocurrencies that prioritize intricate technical frameworks, Dogecoin has gained traction through its relatability and community-driven nature. Musk's support has further amplified its impact, demonstrating how mainstream figures can catalyze interest in decentralized financial tools. His promotion of Dogecoin has encouraged a reexamination of how cryptocurrencies can function not just as speculative assets but as viable means for everyday transactions. This has fueled innovation, pushing developers to create platforms and protocols that incorporate Dogecoin into the expanding world of DeFi, from payment systems to yield farming and decentralized exchanges.

At its core, the intersection of Musk, Dogecoin, and DeFi represents the democratization of finance. Musk's engagement underscores the growing influence of social and cultural factors in shaping financial ecosystems, while Dogecoin exemplifies the potential of humor and relatability to inspire participation. By highlighting these elements, this chapter captures the transformative power of DeFi, not just as a technological revolution but as a cultural shift that challenges conventional ideas of value, trust, and accessibility. In doing so, it invites a deeper conversation about the future of financial systems, where decentralization and inclusivity redefine the parameters of economic participation.

10

The Volatility of Dogecoin

Chapter 9:

Dogecoin's journey in the cryptocurrency world has been marked by dramatic price swings, making it a prime example of the volatility that defines digital currencies. Originating as a meme-inspired cryptocurrency, Dogecoin gained unexpected traction due to its community-driven ethos and celebrity endorsements. Unlike traditional financial assets, Dogecoin lacks intrinsic value, relying instead on social sentiment and market speculation to drive its price. This inherent unpredictability has made it both an exciting and risky choice for investors, as rapid gains are often accompanied by equally sharp declines.

Several factors contribute to Dogecoin's volatility, chief among them being its decentralized nature and lack of a capped supply. Unlike Bitcoin, which has a finite maximum supply, Dogecoin's infinite minting mechanism ensures an ever-expanding circulation, diluting scarcity over time. Additionally, its price is heavily influenced by social media trends and the endorsements of influential figures, creating a feedback loop of hype and sell-offs. The absence of robust utility beyond being a speculative asset further amplifies its susceptibility to market sentiment, making its valuation fragile and reactive to news cycles.

For investors, navigating the volatility of Dogecoin demands a careful balance of optimism and caution. While its meteoric rises can deliver substantial short-term profits, the lack of underlying fundamentals means that crashes are an ever-present risk. It is imperative to approach Dogecoin with a clear strategy, recognizing that its value is shaped more by collective belief than by tangible assets or consistent use cases. Understanding these dynamics is crucial for anyone venturing into the volatile waters of Dogecoin investment, as it underscores the importance of timing, diversification, and informed decision-making in the unpredictable realm of cryptocurrencies.

11

Dogecoin in 2025: Where are we now?

Chapter 10:

As we step into 2025, Dogecoin has transitioned from being a lighthearted meme to a significant presence in the cryptocurrency ecosystem. Originally launched in 2013 as a joke, Dogecoin's rise is a testament to the unpredictable nature of digital currencies. While it began as a fun and quirky alternative to Bitcoin, its widespread use in tipping, charity donations, and microtransactions has gradually earned it recognition. By 2025, Dogecoin's market capitalization has soared, and it is frequently seen alongside established cryptocurrencies like Bitcoin and Ethereum in discussions about the future of digital finance. It has shed much of its initial image and is now regarded as a serious asset, contributing to the shifting perception of what digital currencies can achieve.

The influence of Elon Musk has remained a key factor in Dogecoin's journey. His public support, through social media and statements, has undoubtedly contributed to the coin's visibility and popularity. Musk's involvement goes beyond mere endorsements; his role has spurred ongoing developments in Dogecoin's technology and usability. In 2025, Dogecoin has seen advancements that make it more competitive with other cryptocurrencies, with improvements in scalability and transaction speed. Musk's backing has also opened doors for Dogecoin to integrate into new use cases, such as partnerships with companies accepting it as a form of payment. His vision for Dogecoin continues to shape its trajectory, though the coin's future is not solely tethered to his influence.

Dogecoin's success has wider implications for the future of cryptocurrency. It signals that cryptocurrencies can evolve from niche concepts into mainstream financial tools, despite initial skepticism or unconventional beginnings. The rise of Dogecoin has led to increased adoption of alternative coins, prompting other projects to focus on community-driven development, accessibility, and practical use cases. As governments and financial institutions begin to take cryptocurrency more seriously, the story of Dogecoin in 2025 serves as a reminder that innovation in the digital currency space can emerge from unexpected places. This marks a pivotal moment in the ongoing evolution of decentralized finance, one where even the most unconventional ideas can reshape global economic landscapes.

12

The Future of Digital Finance

Chapter 11:

The rise of digital currencies like Dogecoin has marked a pivotal shift in the financial landscape. While Bitcoin and Ethereum have been dominant forces, newer digital assets such as Dogecoin are gaining recognition. Cryptocurrencies are increasingly seen as a viable alternative to traditional currencies, offering faster transactions, lower fees, and a degree of decentralization that challenges the conventional banking system. As digital currencies become more mainstream, traditional financial institutions are being forced to adapt. We are witnessing banks, investment firms, and payment platforms integrating blockchain technology into their services, blending the old with the new. This convergence promises greater efficiency in global financial transactions, but it also raises important questions about security, regulation, and the role of central authorities.

Blockchain technology is at the heart of this revolution. It offers a decentralized and transparent way of storing data, which is crucial for verifying transactions and ensuring the integrity of digital currencies. The adoption of blockchain extends beyond finance and is being applied in sectors such as supply chain management, healthcare, and even voting systems. This technology promises to disrupt industries by eliminating intermediaries and reducing the potential for fraud. However, blockchain's widespread implementation will face hurdles, particularly concerning scalability and energy consumption. As the demand for faster and more efficient blockchain solutions grows, so too does the challenge of making this technology sustainable and accessible to all users.

Influential figures like Elon Musk have played a significant role in shaping the future of digital finance. Musk's tweets and public endorsements of certain cryptocurrencies, including Dogecoin, have sent shockwaves through the market, often causing price surges and attracting attention from both retail and institutional investors. His involvement has highlighted the intersection of social media, celebrity influence, and financial markets, demonstrating how digital finance is no longer just the domain of traditional investors. As the next decade unfolds, digital currencies and blockchain technology will likely continue to evolve, influenced by innovation, regulation, and the power of public figures. The future of digital finance is dynamic, offering new opportunities and challenges for both investors and regulators alike.

13

The Musk Effect: What We've Learned

Chapter 12: Elon Musk's involvement with Dogecoin has been one of the most remarkable and unpredictable events in the history of digital currencies. Initially launched as a joke, Dogecoin quickly gained momentum when Musk, through his tweets and public statements, fueled its rise to prominence. His ability to capture the public's attention and influence the crypto market has shown just how powerful an individual's voice can be in a decentralized financial system. This episode has highlighted that the cryptocurrency space is more than just about technology; it is also deeply influenced by personalities, media, and social trends. Musk's engagement with Dogecoin illustrated how a single individual could play a pivotal role in the volatility of digital currencies, pushing their value up or down with just a few words.

The broader implications of Musk's involvement in Dogecoin extend far beyond the realm of cryptocurrency itself. His influence has led to a deeper conversation about the relationship between wealth, power, and technology. The rise of digital currencies, powered by figures like Musk, signals a shift in how people view traditional finance and the role of central banks and governments. By supporting Dogecoin, Musk presented a new model of financial freedom where decentralized assets, untethered to the conventional financial system, could potentially challenge the old norms. His actions also raised concerns about market manipulation and the ethics of influential figures engaging with speculative investments, leaving society to question the balance between personal influence and financial responsibility in the modern age.

Looking ahead, the future of Dogecoin and cryptocurrency in general remains uncertain but promising. While Dogecoin's rise was, in part, a result of Musk's playful tweets, the lasting impact may be seen in the broader acceptance and mainstream integration of digital currencies. However, with the volatile nature of these assets, the question arises: can they truly replace traditional currencies, or are they simply a fleeting trend driven by public figures? As influential personalities continue to shape the landscape, it will be essential to consider the long-term consequences of their actions, not just on the value of currencies but also on the financial world at large. The Musk Effect has revealed the profound role that influential figures can play, but the future of cryptocurrency will ultimately depend on how these technologies evolve and how society adapts to their presence in everyday life.

14

Conclusion

In concluding this exploration of *The Musk Effect*, it becomes evident that influence, when wielded by a figure as dynamic as Elon Musk, has the potential to reshape entire industries. Musk's association with Dogecoin transcended the boundaries of conventional finance, turning what began as a lighthearted meme into a cryptocurrency of global significance. This phenomenon illustrates the growing intersection between technology, finance, and social influence, showing how digital platforms can amplify individual voices to create monumental shifts in economic trends.

The rise of Dogecoin underscores the unpredictable and innovative nature of the cryptocurrency landscape. What started as an internet joke quickly transformed into a multi-billion-dollar asset, fueled by Musk's tweets and public endorsements. This evolution challenges traditional notions of value and investment, reminding us that in a digital age, sentiment and momentum can hold as much weight as technical analysis or market fundamentals. It serves as a case study in how the convergence of celebrity influence and digital culture can drive the adoption of financial products, even in unconventional ways.

As we move toward 2025 and beyond, the Dogecoin phenomenon and Musk's broader impact on the crypto world highlight the untapped potential of digital finance. Whether viewed as a speculative bubble or a legitimate form of investment, Dogecoin has demonstrated the power of narrative and community in shaping market behavior. Musk's role in this dynamic will likely remain a blueprint for how innovation and influence can coalesce to redefine the boundaries of global finance. The future is poised for even greater shifts, as the lessons from *The Musk Effect* continue to inform how we understand and engage with the digital economy.

www.ingramcontent.com/pod-product-compliance
Lightning Source LLC
LaVergne TN
LVHW010916090225
803313LV00009B/190